77 FRAGMENTS OF A FAMILIAR RUIN

OTHER WORKS BY THOMAS KING

FICTION

Medicine River

Green Grass, Running Water

One Good Story, That One

Truth and Bright Water

A Short History of Indians in Canada

The Back of the Turtle

DREADFULWATER MYSTERIES

DreadfulWater

The Red Power Murders

Cold Skies

A Matter of Malice

Obsidian (forthcoming in 2020)

NON-FICTION

The Truth About Stories: A Native Narrative

The Inconvenient Indian: A Curious Account of Native People in North America

CHILDREN'S ILLUSTRATED BOOKS

A Coyote Columbus Story, illustrated by William Kent Monkman

Coyote Sings to the Moon, illustrated by Johnny Wales

Coyote's New Suit, illustrated by Johnny Wales

A Coyote Solstice Tale, illustrated by Gary Clement

Coyote Tales, illustrated by Byron Eggenschwiler

77 FRAGMENTS OF A FAMILIAR RUIN

POEMS

THOMAS KING

HarperCollins*PublishersLtd*

77 Fragments of a Familiar Ruin

Published by HarperCollins Publishers Ltd

First edition

HarperCollins Publishers Ltd
Bay Adelaide Centre, East Tower
22 Adelaide Street West, 41st Floor
Toronto, Ontario, Canada
M5H 4E3

www.harpercollins.ca

Library and Archives Canada Cataloguing in Publication information is available upon request.

ISBN 978-1-4434-5944-0

Printed and bound in the United States

LSC/H 9 8 7 6 5 4 3

For my mother, second from the left.
Much more than a fragment.

77 FRAGMENTS OF A FAMILIAR RUIN

1

As for the garden,
  Adam,
  after the Fall.
Make no mistake, he said,
  we will destroy it all.

2

Okay.
Let's try this again.

And so you don't make
  the same mistake twice,
  Adam was just a joke
  the Otters made up
  to annoy the Ducks.

And it was a Turtle,
  please pay attention,
  not a garden.

3

Set the running days in line,
  tie down the wind.

Mark mountains out with minor tones,
  dig up the stories,
  paint the bones,
  the snow is on the ground.

4

And so we're clear,
 in the beginning
 there was nothing.

Just the water.

Okay, so there were water birds
 and some water animals as well.
Okay, and the Turtle.
Okay, okay, and the light in the western heavens
 that was not a star
 but a falling woman
 slicing through the sky
 like a bright knife.

5

I bite my nails.
I fold toilet paper into squares,
  wipe once
  then fold again.

Raccoons no longer rent movies.

At the airport, Americans took my nail file
  but they'll sell guns to anyone.

I should lose weight.

Somewhere a child is being comforted by her father.

On the off-chance the world will end tomorrow,
  I have begun to read the minor poets.

But there is no hope.

6

Coyote goes to the doctor
  to get tested.

You have had Adverse Childhood Experiences,
  says the doctor.

That would explain why I'm so mischievous,
  says Coyote.
That would explain why I don't learn quickly.
That would explain why I can't control my emotions.
That would explain why I mess up the world.

That will be three hundred and thirty dollars,
  says the doctor.

That would explain why I won't pay you,
  says Coyote.

I've had Adverse Childhood Experiences,
  Coyote tells all his friends.

Can they be cured? says Beaver.

Can they be treated? says Bear.

Let's hope you won't be like this
  for the rest of your life, says Turtle.

I'm sure Social Services will be able to help me,
  says Coyote.

All the animals laugh and agree
  that this is one of Coyote's better jokes.

7

Somewhere in space
  a missile platform
  lingers in orbit.

Bored.

Wondering, in its perfect solitude,
  how hard it would be
  to bring down a star.

8

There are no good jobs in the slaughterhouse.
Those with the knives.
Those in the pens.

In the slaughterhouse,
  once the killing begins,
  everyone is covered in blood.

9

On that day
I sit with my mother,
take photographs out of the box,
arrange them on the kitchen table
in order.

Your grandfather, she says,
touching the old black-and-white.
You followed him up the ladder.
He was cleaning gutters.
I took the picture.

And here in the garden
you sitting with him,
the tomatoes ripe and ready.

And again, robbing him in your cowboy hat,
stick horse, wooden gun,
him with his hands in the air,
all for a dime and his love.

There was more to his life than this,
my mother tells me,
but this is all you have,
all you will ever have.
Slips and scraps.
Slivers and shards.
Who you are, who they were.
I am here too,
somewhere.

Can you find what remains?

She puts the photos back in the box,
  closes her eyes,
  sleeps as only the old can sleep,
  sunshine spilling into the room,
  pooling at her feet.

I know this box,
  have sorted through the faces before,
  relations and strangers
  alike,
  fragments of a familiar ruin.

My mother wakes,
  reaches in,
  brings the photograph to light.

Your grandmother,
  she says.

This time
  let us begin
  with her.

10

Nothing passes for favour here.
All talk is razor-toothed.
Take nothing from the hand
  that offers friendship.
In this place,
  all promises are bruises
  in good suits.

11

Each evening on Chesterman Beach
  the houses that have eaten the forest
  wait in the fog
  above the line of the tide
  for the waves
  to come within reach.

12

So I go searching for Superman
  on the internet
  and stumble across the neutron bomb
  that destroys hard targets
  faster than a speeding bullet.

By which they mean me.

And leaves soft targets intact,
  in a single bound.

By which they mean
  private property.

I lift up mine eyes unto the sky,
  whence cometh my help,
  and hope all I see
  is a bird.

13

All the dreams are empty now.

Check back in May.

14

The thing about
  the abyss
  is that the view
  doesn't improve
  the closer you get
  to the edge.

15

Ring the bells that go cha-ching.
Discard your moral posturings.
Walmart discounts everything.
That's how the blight begins.

16

At the concert,
  women with horns and drums,
  men with guitars and keyboards,
  play music that ends poverty
  and protects the environment.

Why are they so young?

The trumpet has a fourth valve,
  I hear someone say,
  as though it's
  a thumb
  on a snake.

How do they do it?
Play apart.
Play together.
In tune.

Let's send them to Ottawa.
To Washington and Moscow,
  to Beijing and Berlin,
  to Walmart and Royal Dutch Shell,
  to British Petroleum and Amazon,
  anywhere decisions about people
  and the planet are made.

Parliaments, Congresses,
  Senates, Corporate Boards,
  Central Committees.
  All the dusty chamber pots of power,
  tip them on end and bang the bottoms,
  shake out the toads
  (these are not frogs to be kissed)

Shake them out
  kick them to the curb,
  these destroyers of worlds.

Give them a stick and a Timmy cup.
See if they can keep time
  better than they kept the peace.

Turn the world over to musicians.
  Brass and strings,
  reeds and percussion,
  choir optional.

Orchestra rules.
Congenial four-four scores
  inside the stave
  so everyone can play.

17

Oh,
  and the Woman Who Fell From the Sky?
Her name wasn't Eve,
  it was Evening.
And she was pregnant.

Though you could have figured
  that out for yourself
  if you had taken the time
  to look.

18

At the powwow,
  the women stand behind the drum
  and sing.

These are no ordinary women,
  no ordinary voices.
Mountains move.
Tides retreat.
Stars fall.

You've been warned.

Stand away and let them pass.
Stand away and let them pass.

19

Imagine I've written you
  a love poem.

Imagine how it might
  sound in a warm wind,
  feel in a long caress,
  look waking up together
  in the morning.

Imagine I've written you
  a love poem.

See.

That wasn't so hard.

20

Why tolerate such gods as these,
  so stern and crucified with pain?
Why not a gentler touch demand?
A kinder world,
  a peaceful earth
  to hold us at a second birth.

No judgements needed in that hour.
No promised paradise, no flame.

Our jangling past of fears and dreams
  already left behind us.
Leave us be.
Leave us be.
To find our own way round again,
  amidst the dust and warming rain.

21

For the houses braced behind the gates,
each new day brings
the threat
of community.

22 Shopping is good.

23

Raven goes to Ottawa
  to see the Prime Minister.

I wouldn't make this up.

Boy, am I glad to see you,
  the Prime Minister tells Raven,
  maybe you can help us with
  our Indian problem.

Sure, says Raven,
  what's the problem?

When Otter tells the story,
  he always laughs
  and spoils the ending.

24

Perhaps the pandemic
that will destroy humankind
is longevity.

25

Coyote goes to the doctor
  to get tested.

You don't have Adverse Childhood Experiences,
  says the doctor.
You're just spirited.

That would explain why I'm so mischievous,
  says Coyote.
That would explain why I don't learn things quickly.
That would explain why I can't control my emotions.
That would explain why I mess up the world.

That will be three hundred and thirty dollars,
  says the doctor.

That's the spirit, says Coyote.

I'm spirited,
  Coyote tells all his friends.

You certainly are, says Beaver.

Want to hear me shout? says Coyote.

Maybe you could be a little less spirited, says Bear.

Want to watch me bang my head against a wall?
  says Coyote.

You don't want to be like this the rest of your life,
  says Turtle.

Yes, I do, says Coyote. Yesidoyesidoyesido.

The animals draw straws to see who gets
  to call Social Services.

26

Each week
  on network television
  hundreds of terrorist attacks
  are thwarted
  by members
  of the Actors Guild.

Perhaps they could visit
  schools
  when they're not
  on set.

27 Let us now celebrate prisons.

28

The Woman Who Fell From the Sky
  sits on the back of the Turtle
  and looks down into the water.

The first thing we need, she says,
  is dry land
  and to make dry land
  we need mud
  and the mud we need
  is down there.

29

When I get frustrated
  I go to the river
  and throw rocks
  at the water.

That's me.

Other people bomb cities.

30

Tonight I'll watch the game,
  watch men take war
  for spectacle and sport.

Full contact.

There on the flandering fields
  traced out in shadow
  and in light
  surrounded by the faithful,
  opening night.

Cheerleaders.
Vendors.
Pennants flying.
How we love to celebrate
  the dying
  from the safety of the stands.
The marching bands strike up
  a corporate refrain
  while Prime-Time Prophets rise and shine
  for anthems and transactional acclaim.

And then.

And then with all the cheering and the singing,
  with all the shouts of righteousness still ringing
  in our ears
  the game begins.

31

Baby seals playing in tidal pools
  on Wharariki Beach,
  South Island, New Zealand,
  have decided not to
  invade Iran.

I no longer fly.

Pocahontas never slept with John Smith.
He made the whole thing up,
  knowing that memory is no more
  than a series of well-told stories
  told often.

No one can tell me why
  fresh produce comes sealed in plastic,
  or why an aspirin costs more than a bullet.

I can still see the stars at night,
  but there is no hope.

32

Why would we want something
  after death?

As though life weren't enough
  and now
  at the end
  we expect a reward
  for all the joys and sufferings?

Eternal life?
Really?

Paradise?
You're kidding.

Spend eternity basking in the warmth
  of the Sun?

Please.
Nobody stays on the beach for more than a week.

33

A long drive on a dark road.
Minutes into years.
No low-mileage life, this one.
Stopping only for bathrooms and food,
  lovers and children,
  a flat tire.
Memories in the mirror.
No destination in sight.
Foot on the pedal.
Eyes on the road.

34

Let us now discuss
  missing and
  murdered
  aboriginal women.

Let us now discuss
  murdered
  aboriginal women.

Let us now discuss
   aboriginal women.

Let us now discuss.

35

Dr. Charles Eastman
  rides From the Deep Woods to Civilization
  just in time to greet
  the first wagon back from
  Big Foot's camp.

My Lai Rosewood Jallianwala Delhi

Skeptical,
  he leaves the fort
  to dispel for himself
  the rumour of ghosts
  dancing on the land.

Montreal Hiroshima Treblinka Qana

While all around,
  Custer's Seventh,
  mad for Weapons of Mass Destruction
  and genocidal glory,
  gallops the world
  in hot pursuit of peace.

Sand Creek Carthage Rwanda Tiananmen Square

But there,
  on the frozen plains,
  South Dakota, December 29, 1890,
  searching for survivors,
  Eastman finds nothing
  save the future.

36

To reconcile, here's what to do.
The rules are simple,
  the rules are few.

Honour the promises,
  do what you say,
  restore the land
  and get out of our way.

Send the lawyers to
  another dance,
  and keep your apologies
  in your pants.

37

A contest, shout the Ducks.
  It's a contest.

No need to push,
  says Evening,
  everyone will get a turn.

So one by one
  the water animals line up
  to see who will be the first
  to find the mud.

38

Raven votes for herself
  and becomes Prime Minister.

How could this happen,
  ask the animals.

It's easy, says Raven.
When no one is paying attention,
  anything is possible.

39

That night at the powwow,
  the men around the big drum
  sing heyya, heyya, heyya,
  to bring the women close.

While the grandmothers sit
  in folding chairs
  and shout to the dancers.

Don't be misled, they call out.
Those men can't sing.
The drum is a ventriloquist.

40

We live in hardening times.

Soft men bring down the heavens
  with their lies.

Planets turn.
Bushes burn.

For those of us who live to take
  no sacrifice becomes too great
  for someone else's child to make.

Bushes burn.
Planets turn.

Soft men bring down the heavens
  with their lies.

We live in hardening times.

41

Let us not mention love.

Let us talk about food instead.

I could remind you to take the tissues
out of your pockets
before I do
the laundry.

You could remind me which bin
is for dental floss.

We might consider a trip
somewhere warm
once the treatments end.

Perhaps we'll walk along the river
or lie on the floor with pillows
and put photographs
in order.

But let us not mention love.

42

In Alberta
  the sour gas wells
  rise out of the land
  like candles on a cake.

Make a wish. Blow them out.
Make a wish. Blow them out.

43

Vatican City is sold to a
  wholly owned subsidiary of
  Monsanto.

Mecca is repossessed
  for unpaid debts
  and put up for auction
  on eBay.

In Washington, DC
  the World Bank is selling
  fresh air
  in cans.

Today I plan to get out of bed.

But there is no hope.

44

The first animal to dive
  into the water
  is Duck.

Duck is gone for a long time
  and when she floats to the surface,
  she doesn't have any mud.

It's dark down there, she says,
  and cold
  and lonely.

Okay, says the Woman Who Fell From the Sky,
  who wants to go next?

45

Go back
  and read the first
  forty-four fragments
  again.

I'll wait.

46 No, really,
I'll wait.

47

After Raven steals the sun,
  she steals the water,
  seals it in plastic bottles,
  sells it for a profit.

So, that's where all our
  water went,
  say the animals.

Yes, says Raven,
  now
  you
  know.

48

Coyote goes to the doctor
to get tested.

There's nothing wrong with you,
says the doctor.
You're just a total _____ up.

That would explain why I'm so mischievous,
says Coyote.
That would explain why I don't learn things quickly.
That would explain why I can't control my emotions.
That would explain why I mess up the world.

That will be three hundred and thirty dollars,
says the doctor.

_____ off, says Coyote.

I'm a total _____ up,
  Coyote tells all his friends.

You're not that bad, says Beaver.

_____ you, says Coyote.

And you're our friend, says Bear.

_____ you too, says Coyote.

We just want you to be happy, says Turtle.

And _____ Social Services, says Coyote.

All the animals agree that
  the professionals at Social Services
  will be able to fill in the blanks.

49

Under the new moon,
the old Indian
lies in wait
by the side of the road.

When the police arrive
he has already field-dressed
a Dodge Ram
and a Volkswagen Rabbit.

Treaty rights, he tells the court,
subsistence hunting.

The judge gives him thirty days
for poaching,
lectures him on the sanctity
of private property,
asks if he thinks the Stampeders
will make the playoffs.

Later, in jail, he teaches inmates
  how to stalk the Ford Broncos
  overgrazing the Trans-Canada
  and what to do when faced
  with an irate Mustang
  in a Costco parking lot.

You ever bring down a Jaguar?

No point, the old Indian tells the caged men.
They're in the shop all the time
  and there's not enough meat
  on the F-type to feed a family
  for more than a day.

50

Early one morning
and the whole lot of rugged
god-fearing heroes
fresh from the splendour
of the Old World
arrive in the New,
row away from the ships,
leap into the surf and stride ashore.
Flagged and garlanded,
full of song and sweet words,
they greet the dumbfounded savages
who wait naked on the shore,
desperate to receive the gifts of civilization.

Or

Early one morning
and the whole lot of arrogant
religious bigots
run out of the Old World for cause
arrive in the New,
sneak up in rowboats,
flounder in the surf and stumble ashore.
Fouled and danked,
skunked and sweated,
full of vice and eager greed,
they greet the Americans
who wait on the shore,
ready to share the gifts of civilization
with these dissolute and pitiful creatures.

Or

Make up your own damn story.

51

The next animal
  is Loon.

I'll find the mud, he says,
  and he dives deep into the water.

But when he comes to the surface
  his mouth is empty.
It's there, he says,
  but I can't reach it.

52

(to be performed with a fiddle and a double bass)

Howdy partner,
  my name's Bill.
Welcome to the dance on Parliament Hill.
Grab your sweetie
  and make a square,
  leave your ethics over there.
Bow to the banks and the corporations,
  show them our appreciation.
Promenade and stomp your feet,
  lie to everyone you meet.
Shelter all your dough-see-dough
  in a tropical bank
  where the law won't go.
Roll away in a half sashay
  'cause climate change
  is here to stay.
Circle left, circle right,
  wave to the voters
  and say good night.

Note: Dancers are expected to make promises they don't intend to keep. Paying the caller and the musicians a living wage is optional.

53

The two of them searching for bird eggs
  on the western shore.
She doesn't ask if he loves her,
  knows better,
  wants him to find the story
  on his own.

She takes off her clothes and moves
  naked across the crags,
  the birds scuttling away,
  as she climbs
  closing in behind,
  keeping the distance fixed.

Will he follow?

At the top of the cliff, she waits.
The spray on her breasts,
  half-light, salt, and the scent
  of longing.

Don't read between the lines,
  she says,
  as he reaches her side,
  knowing all the while that this is where
  the best stories hide.

54

How came we to this
  fantasy of god?
What fears do such
  a fatal notion ease?
Was Falling such a consummate disgrace
  that we would leave compassion
  at the gate
  and come into this world
  indignant and undone,
  desperate for salvation?

Or are we but assassins by trade,
  undeterred by nature's grace,
  content to let all kindness fall,
  burn down the tower,
  storm the garden wall.

55

Caution.

All gods are to be
  constructed
  out of something
  inflexible
  so they will not bend
  in the wind.

56

The trick, she said,
  is to bend in the wind
  without
  falling over.

57

In the New Times, you say,
  I won't have to spend my nights
  standing at the edge of Saskatoon,
  watching frozen skies
  alone.

Can you see me?
I can see you.
There, in the house,
  the windows warm and yawning
  in golden light.

In the New Times
  you'll call out to tell me of a bed,
  of a chair,
  of a place at the table.

Come to the porch.
Come to the porch.
No need to force the door.

It's open.

In the New Times,
  when we recall January 2000,
  we'll smile and say
  that it was most likely
  the wind
  that caused the problems.
Or the slope of the land.
Or the sound of winter thunder.

In the New Times
  we'll agree,
  won't we,
  that it wasn't you
  and it wasn't me,
  wasn't even the blood words
  no one uses anymore.

It was the cold stars,
  surely.
Not that it matters.

Or perhaps it was the black road
  that pours out across the land
  like a flood.

Or the dark cruiser that brought me
  to such a place
  on such a night
  to wait for the New Times to come.

58

Tell me.
Tell me, who is left to hate?
Surely there is someone new,
  someone missed
  the first time through.

Tell me.
Shall we circle round
  and bring our wicked selves
  to ground?

Tell me.
Tell me.

59

Raven stands on the street corner
  and sells authentic Indian jewellery.

It's all so lovely, says a woman with a dog,
  but how do I know it's authentic?

That's easy, says Raven.
Authentic Indian jewellery
  has *Taiwan* stamped on the bottom.

Really, says the woman with the dog.

Oh, yes, says Raven.
Of course, this wasn't always true.
In the old days,
  all the good stuff
  said *Japan*.

60

Coyote goes to the doctor
  to get tested.

Your problem,
  says the doctor,
  is that no one likes you.

That would explain why I'm so mischievous,
  says Coyote.
That would explain why I don't learn quickly.
That would explain why I can't control my emotions.
That would explain why I mess up the world.

That will be three hundred and thirty dollars,
  says the doctor.

That would explain why I don't like myself.

No one likes me,
  Coyote tells all his friends.

I like you, says Beaver.

Do you like me when I yell at you?

I like you, says Bear.

Do you like me when I hit you?

I like you, says Turtle.

I'm going to jump into the ocean,
  says Coyote,
  sink to the bottom
  and never come up.

The animals call Social Services,
  where the wait time is longer than usual
  due to increased volume.

61

Float me,
  float me on the water,
  in the pools at the turn of the tide.
Let me drift with the winds
  in the margins
  and rest in the peace
  love provides.

Too old for the land.
Too young for the sea.
When I die,
  cradle me
  in the sunlit shallows of memory.

Float me,
  float me on the water.

62

So, one by one the animals
dive to the bottom
of the water
to try to find the mud.

And they fail.

If I don't have mud,
says Evening,
I can't make the earth.

And just then Raven flies in.
What's with all the water, she says.
I thought we'd have some
dry land by now.

A water world isn't all that bad,
say the Ducks.

In fact, it's perfect,
say the Fish.

We could certainly do a whole lot worse,
say the Otters.

And as the animals argue,
the water begins to bubble
and Turtle begins to shake.

Uh-oh, says Raven,
looks as though Evening is
going into labour.

63

There is a changing at each dawn
  that only dying people see,
  that rides the air
  and narrow light,
  a twinkling,
  quickly,
  then a plunge.

And in that moment,
  in that brief refrain,
  all is water,
  all is falling rain.

64

On Monday,
executives at Nestlé
decide to stop
draining
aquifers.

On Wednesday,
  Parliament votes
  to honour treaties
  made with Indigenous Peoples.

Today,
  there are reports
  of flying pigs
  on final approach
  into Pearson International.

But there is no hope.

65

But
in my grandfather's garden,
I am the best boy
in the world.

66 Immigrant settlers and Indian land.
Railroads and highways and Indian land.
Resource extraction and Indian land.
Nuclear waste dumps and Indian land.
Hydroelectric and Indian land.
Pipelines and pipelines and Indian land.

Tell me again
  what you don't understand.

Tell me again
  what you don't understand.

67

Attending the wedding
in spite of everything
I know about
funerals.

68

My uncle savages the streets,
skates figure eights
around the meters,
drums the cars.

He gimmes change from laughing folk
in tight white skins
and sheepy coats,
round dances round the block
in red face,
clown-crows out the words he carries
on his cuffs.

Until the cops come
and chauffeur him away
with Marvin and the rest
to Burger King.
A break.
Union rules.

Tough job, he says to Marvin
over fries, but hey,
someone has to hold the middle class
in line
and keep them from the woods.

69

In most of the paintings you see,
  Custer is standing in a pile of bodies,
  firing his pistol and waving his sword
  around the whole of Montana.

He has long hair in the one
  that hangs over the bar in Great Falls
  and it looks as though
  he is laughing with the dead men
  at his feet.

But in the original,
  Custer has a crew cut,
  sits on his horse,
  squints at a map,
  lost in the heart of the heart of the country,
  when he hears someone yell,
  By god, we've got them now!

And as he turns in the saddle
  to see what all the damn shouting
  is about,
  he is hit in the ear
  by a stray ricochet
  and dies mid-sentence.

What he was about to say is,
  fortunately,
  of little consequence.

70

We see those ones coming,
three, four hundred years away.

We're poets, they say,
but we can see the guns
under their coats.

Watch this, they say,
as they shoot at road signs
from pickup trucks and minivans.

We turn our backs,
embarrassed.

We can help you,
they shout.

But we know what they want.

We're okay, we tell them.
We're comfortable in our own imaginations,
tell our own stories,
sing our own songs.

No, no, the poets cry and wave their guns,
you need our help!

Go away, we tell them,
but they just hang around
looking for something else
to shoot.

71 Directive for Entrenching Indigenous Rights:

Soft ground.
A shovel.

72 I'm not going into labour, says Evening,
and she leans over and looks deep into the water
and what she sees is a brown blur
streaking to the surface.

Watch out! she shouts, and then water explodes.

And up pops Coyote
with a human being
in his mouth.

Raven shakes the water off her wings.
Now that, she says, is something
you don't see every day.

Hello, says Coyote,
I'm looking for Social Services.

Uh-oh, says Evening, this is not what I had in mind.

No, says Raven,
I don't think this is the story
you wanted to tell.

73

How could such a beginning
ringed in water,
come to such an end
fixed in fire?

74

Coyote takes the human being out of his mouth
  and places it on the back of the Turtle.

Where did you find THAT? say the Ducks.

In the mud at the bottom of the water,
  says Coyote.

Swell, says Raven, but what are we
  supposed to do with it?

What I want to know, shouts Evening,
  as the first contractions hit,
  is where you two came from
  and
  how you got into this story.

75

With all that we could do,
  we do this?

With all that
  we
  could do,
  we do this?

With all that
  we
  could do,
  we
  do
  this.

76

Evening gives birth to twins.
A girl
  and a boy.

It's going to get crowded,
  says Raven.

You might want to consider
  something larger
  than Turtle,
  says Coyote.

If someone would get me some mud,
  says Evening,
  I could make a world.

How about a garden, says Coyote.
A garden would be a swell idea.

Okay, says Evening,
  it would appear
  we're going to have
  to start this story
  all over.

Again.

77

So in the beginning
there was nothing.

Just the water.